Shabbat

A
Family
Service

By Judith Z. Abrams
Illustrated by Katherine Janus Kahn

KAR-BEN
PUBLISHING

JUDITH Z. ABRAMS is rabbi of Congregation Beth El in Missouri City, TX. A graduate of Oberlin College, she was ordained at the Hebrew Union College-Jewish Institute of Religion in 1985, and has served in congregations in Ohio, Illinois, and Virginia. In addition to Shabbat and High Holiday services for children, she has written the *Talmud for Beginners* series for adults.

KATHERINE JANUS KAHN, Maryland artist, calligrapher, and sculptor, has illustrated an impressive list of Jewish books for children, including the *Sammy Spider* series, *The Hardest Word, A Family Haggadah,* and a series of toddler board books.

Also by Judith Abrams and Katherine Kahn:

Selichot: A Family Service
Rosh Hashanah: A Family Service
Yom Kippur: A Family Service
Sukkot: A Family Seder
Simchat Torah: A Family Celebration with Consecration Service

Text copyright © 1991 by Judith Z. Abrams
Illustrations copyright © 1991 by Katherine Janus Kahn

KAR-BEN PUBLISHING, INC.
A division of Lerner Publishing Group
241 First Avenue North
Minneapolis, MN 55401 U.S.A.
800-4KARBEN

Website address: www.karben.com

Library of Congress Cataloging-in-Publication Data

Abrams, Judith Z.
    Shabbat: a family service/Judith Z. Abrams; illustrated by Katherine Janus Kahn.
      p. cm.
    Summary: A family service for the Jewish Sabbath.
    ISBN: 0-929371-29-1
    1. Sabbath—Liturgy—Texts—Juvenile literature. 2. Judaism—Liturgy—Texts—Juvenile literature. [1. Sabbath. 2. Judaism—Liturgy.] I. Kahn, Katherine, ill. II. title.
    BM675.S3Z685 1991
    296.4'1—dc20   91-31640

Manufactured in the United States of America
6 7 8 9 10 11 – JR – 09 08 07 06 05 04

For Michael and Ruth
—JZA

To David
and to Robert
—KJK

WE WELCOME SHABBAT IN SONG

Choose one or more.

Bim Bam, Shabbat Shalom.
A peaceful Shabbat.

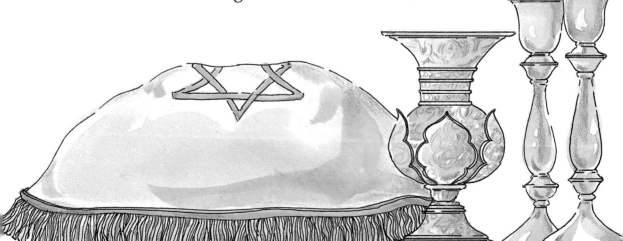

Mah yafeh hayom, Shabbat Shalom.
A lovely day, a peaceful Shabbat.

Lecha dodi likrat kalah p'nei Shabbat n'kabelah.
Let us welcome Shabbat as we greet a beautiful bride.

BLESSING THE SHABBAT CANDLES

On Friday evening.

בָּרוּךְ אַתָּה יְיָ אֱלֹהֵינוּ מֶלֶךְ הָעוֹלָם
אֲשֶׁר קִדְּשָׁנוּ בְּמִצְוֹתָיו וְצִוָּנוּ לְהַדְלִיק נֵר שֶׁל שַׁבָּת.

Baruch Atah Adonai, Eloheinu Melech ha'olam,
Asher kid'shanu b'mitzvotav v'tzivanu l'hadlik ner shel Shabbat.

Blessed are You, Adonai our God,
Ruler of the World
Who makes us holy through Your mitzvot
And commands us to light the Shabbat candles.

WHAT IS SHABBAT?

Shabbat is a special day of the week.

On
Sunday and
Monday and
Tuesday and
Wednesday and
Thursday and
Friday

we are busy learning, growing,
playing, and building.

Shabbat begins Friday at sunset.
On Shabbat we create a special day to share
with family and friends.

We create it with
candles and challah,
wine and song,
Torah and prayer.

We begin by blessing God's name.
We rise.

בָּרְכוּ אֶת־יְיָ הַמְבֹרָךְ.
בָּרוּךְ יְיָ הַמְבֹרָךְ לְעוֹלָם וָעֶד.

Barechu et Adonai hamevorach!
Baruch Adonai hamevorach le'olam va'ed!

Bless Adonai Who is to be blessed!
Blessed is Adonai forever!
We sit down.

We thank God for the world around us.
God is everywhere, and God is One.

We thank God for the sun and stars.
God is everywhere, and God is One.

We thank God for giving us the Torah.
God is everywhere, and God is One.

We thank God for family and friends.
God is everywhere, and God is One.

When we say the *Shema*, we are saying,
God is everywhere, and God is One.

THE
SHEMA

שְׁמַע יִשְׂרָאֵל יְיָ אֱלֹהֵינוּ יְיָ אֶחָד.

Shema Yisrael Adonai Eloheinu Adonai Echad.

Listen, O Israel, Adonai is our God, Adonai Alone.

בָּרוּךְ שֵׁם כְּבוֹד מַלְכוּתוֹ לְעוֹלָם וָעֶד.

Baruch shem k'vod malchuto l'olam va'ed:

Blessed is Adonai Who rules forever.

וְאָהַבְתָּ אֵת יְיָ אֱלֹהֶיךָ בְּכָל־לְבָבְךָ וּבְכָל־נַפְשְׁךָ וּבְכָל־מְאֹדֶךָ.

V'ahavta et Adonai Elohecha b'chol l'vavcha,
uv'chol nafshecha uv'chol m'odecha.

WE

will love God
with all our heart
and all our might.
Now and in the future,
at home and away,
from morning until night,
God's words will guide how we live.

GOD

has guided us throughout our long history.

God created the world for us,
Rescued us from slavery in Egypt,
And gave us rules to live by.

Whenever we remember how good God has been to us,
we sing this song:

מִי־כָמֹכָה בָּאֵלִם יְיָ מִי־כָמֹכָה נֶאְדָּר בַּקֹּדֶשׁ
נוֹרָא תְהִלֹּת עֹשֵׂה פֶלֶא.

Mi chamocha ba'elim Adonai. Mi kamocha ne'dar bakodesh.
Nora tehilot, oseh feleh.

Who is like You, Adonai?
You are mighty, You perform wonders.

11

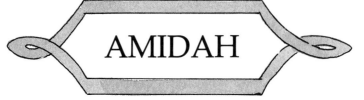

AMIDAH

בָּרוּךְ אַתָּה יְיָ אֱלֹהֵינוּ וֵאלֹהֵי אֲבוֹתֵינוּ וְאִמּוֹתֵינוּ, אֱלֹהֵי
אַבְרָהָם, יִצְחָק, וְיַעֲקוֹב, אֱלֹהֵי שָׂרָה, רִבְקָה, רָחֵל, וְלֵאָה.

*Baruch Atah Adonai Eloheinu, Elohei avoteinu v'imoteinu, Elohei
Avraham, Yitzchak, v'Yaakov, Elohei Sarah, Rivkah, Rachel, v'Leah.*

Blessed are You, God of our fathers and mothers,
God of Abraham, Isaac, and Jacob,
God of Sarah, Rebecca, Rachel, and Leah.
God Who is high up in the heavens,
Yet close enough to hear us.

| Abraham and Sarah | Isaac and Rebecca | Jacob, Leah, and Rachel |

God of our past, God of our future,
  You bless us with Shabbat joy.

You created the world and then You rested.
  You bless us with Shabbat rest.

You called Shabbat a holy day.
  You bless us with Shabbat holiness.

You gave us Shabbat as a gift for all time.
  You bless us with Shabbat peace.

We can make this a Shabbat Shalom in many ways:

> *By not fighting with our families.*
> *By sharing with our friends.*
> *By caring for those around us.*

בָּרוּךְ אַתָּה יְיָ הַמְבָרֵךְ אֶת־עַמּוֹ יִשְׂרָאֵל בַּשָּׁלוֹם.

Baruch Atah Adonai hamevarech et amo Yisrael bashalom.

Thank You God,
for giving us these paths to peace.

We pause for a
SILENT PRAYER

We sing.
*Oseh shalom bimromav, Hu ya'aseh shalom
aleinu v'al kol Yisrael v'imru AMEN.*
May God who makes peace in the heavens bring
peace to us and the world. AMEN.

TORAH SERVICE

On Shabbat we read the Torah and tell stories about our big family, the Jewish people.

We rise as we take the Torah from the Ark and sing:

Ki mitzion tetzei Torah, u'dvar Adonai Mirushalayim.
The Torah will come from Zion, and God's word from Jerusalem.

שְׁמַע יִשְׂרָאֵל יְיָ אֱלֹהֵינוּ יְיָ אֶחָד

Shema Yisrael Adonai Eloheinu Adonai Echad.
Listen, O Israel, Adonai is our God, Adonai Alone.
God is One. Holy and awesome is God's Name.

We sit down.

Blessing before reading the Torah:

בָּרְכוּ אֶת-יְיָ הַמְבֹרָךְ.

בָּרוּךְ יְיָ הַמְבֹרָךְ לְעוֹלָם וָעֶד.

בָּרוּךְ אַתָּה יְיָ אֱלֹהֵינוּ מֶלֶךְ הָעוֹלָם אֲשֶׁר בָּחַר-

בָּנוּ מִכָּל הָעַמִּים, וְנָתַן לָנוּ אֶת תּוֹרָתוֹ.

בָּרוּךְ אַתָּה יְיָ נוֹתֵן הַתּוֹרָה.

Barechu et Adonai hamevorach!
Baruch Adonai hamevorach l'olam va'ed!
Baruch Atah Adonai Eloheinu Melech ha'olam asher bachar banu mikol ha'amim,
venatan lanu et Torato. Baruch Atah Adonai, noten hatorah.

Blessed are You, Adonai our God, Ruler of the world,
Who chose us and gave us the Torah.

TORAH READING
OR STORYTIME

Blessing after reading the Torah:

בָּרוּךְ אַתָּה יְיָ אֱלֹהֵינוּ מֶלֶךְ הָעוֹלָם
אֲשֶׁר נָתַן לָנוּ תּוֹרַת אֱמֶת
וְחַיֵּי עוֹלָם נָטַע בְּתוֹכֵנוּ.
בָּרוּךְ אַתָּה יְיָ נוֹתֵן הַתּוֹרָה.

*Baruch Atah Adonai, Eloheinu Melech
ha'olam, asher natan lanu Torat emet
vechayei olam nata b'tochenu. Baruch
Atah Adonai, noten hatorah.*

Blessed are You, Adonai,
Giver of Torah.

We rise as we return the Torah to the Ark and sing:

*Etz chayim hi, l'machazikim bah.
Vetom'cheha me'ushar.
Deracheha, darchei no'am,
Vechol netivoteha shalom.*

The Torah is a tree of life
When we hold it close.
Its ways are pleasant and peaceful.

15

LOOKING BACK
LOOKING AHEAD

On Shabbat, we remember last week and look forward to the week ahead.

We have prayers we say when something important has happened to us and to our family and friends.

Choose those which apply:

For someone who is sick:

May God Who blessed Abraham, Isaac, and Jacob; Sarah, Rebecca, Rachel, and Leah, heal _____ who is sick and restore him/her to good health.

For those who are celebrating a birthday or happy event:

Blessed are You, Adonai our God, Ruler of the World. Who has kept us alive and brought us to this happy time.

For someone who has survived danger:

Blessed are You,
Adonai our God,
Ruler of the World,
Who has shown me
every kindness.

The congregation responds:

May God always be kind to you.

If a new month begins in the coming week:

The new month of _____
will begin on _____.
May it come to us
for life and peace,
for gladness and joy.

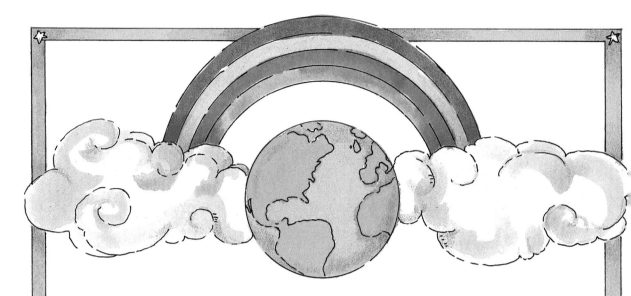

*We join together in a prayer
for our world.*

*May God bless our country and Israel.
May God grant wisdom to our leaders.
May all the peoples of the world know peace.*

ALEINU

We rise.

עָלֵינוּ לְשַׁבֵּחַ לַאֲדוֹן הַכֹּל.

Aleinu leshabeach la'adon hakol.

Let us praise God, Who created this world and created us.
Together, we will work for the day when the whole
world is one and at peace.

וַאֲנַחְנוּ כּוֹרְעִים וּמִשְׁתַּחֲוִים וּמוֹדִים

לִפְנֵי מֶלֶךְ מַלְכֵי הַמְּלָכִים הַקָּדוֹשׁ בָּרוּךְ הוּא.

*Va'anachnu kor'im u'mishtachavim u'modim
Lifnei melech malchei hamelachim, Hakadosh Baruch Hu.*

בַּיּוֹם הַהוּא יִהְיֶה יְיָ אֶחָד וּשְׁמוֹ אֶחָד.

Bayom hahu, bayom hahu, yihiyeh Adonai echad u'shmo echad.

We sit down.

18

KADDISH

On Shabbat we think of all the people we love,
    Those who are with us,
    And those who are not.
We remember the happy times we shared with them,
And the many things they taught us.

We thank God for the time we had together by saying:

יְהֵא שְׁמֵהּ רַבָּא מְבָרַךְ לְעָלַם וּלְעָלְמֵי עָלְמַיָּא.

Yehei sh'mei raba m'varach l'olam ul'almei almaya.
May God's name be praised forever and ever.

FAMILY BLESSING

We ask God's blessing for our family.

יְבָרֶכְךָ יְיָ וְיִשְׁמְרֶךָ.
יָאֵר יְיָ פָּנָיו אֵלֶיךָ וִיחֻנֶּךָּ.
יִשָּׂא יְיָ פָּנָיו אֵלֶיךָ וְיָשֵׂם לְךָ שָׁלוֹם.

Y'vareche'cha Adonai v'yishmerecha.
Ya'er Adonai panav elecha vichuneka.
Yisa Adonai panav elecha, v'yasem l'cha shalom.

May God bless you and keep you.
May God watch over you in kindness.
May God grant you peace.

19

CLOSING SONGS

Choose one or more:

EIN k'Eloheinu, ein k'Adonenu,
Ein k'malkenu, ein k'moshienu.
MI... NODEH... BARUCH... ATAH HU...

None is like our God. We give thanks and bless our God.

❧⟨◎॥◎⟩❧

ADON OLAM, asher malach, b'terem kol yetzir nivra.
L'et na'asah b'cheftzo kol, azai melech sh'mo nikra.

Adonai was our ruler even before the world was created.
Adonai will be our ruler forever.

❧⟨◎॥◎⟩❧

YIGDAL Elohim chai v'yishtabach nimtza v'ein et el m'tzi'uto.
Echad v'ein yachid k'yichudo ne'lam v'gam ein sof l'achduto.

Praised be the living God forever.

❧⟨◎॥◎⟩❧

SHABBAT SHALOM umevorach.

A blessed and peaceful Shabbat.

❧⟨◎॥◎⟩❧

We have made Shabbat special with prayer and song.
Now we make it special with wine and challah.

KIDDUSH AND MOTZI

Raise the cup of wine.

בָּרוּךְ אַתָּה יְיָ

אֱלֹהֵינוּ מֶלֶךְ הָעוֹלָם

בּוֹרֵא פְּרִי הַגָּפֶן.

Baruch Atah Adonai
Eloheinu Melech Ha'olam,
Borei p'ri hagafen.

Blessed are You,
Adonai our God,
Ruler of the World.
Who creates the fruit
of the vine.

Drink the wine.

Uncover the challah.

בָּרוּךְ אַתָּה יְיָ אֱלֹהֵינוּ מֶלֶךְ הָעוֹלָם

הַמּוֹצִיא לֶחֶם מִן הָאָרֶץ.

Baruch Atah Adonai Eloheinu Melech ha'olam.
Hamotzi lechem min ha'aretz.

Blessed are You, Adonai our God,
Ruler of the World.
Who brings bread out of the earth.

Share the challah.

HAVDALAH

We say goodbye to Shabbat with a service called Havdalah. Havdalah means "the difference." Havdalah marks the difference between Shabbat and the rest of the week.

Raise spice box:

בָּרוּךְ אַתָּה יְיָ
אֱלֹהֵינוּ מֶלֶךְ הָעוֹלָם
בּוֹרֵא מִינֵי בְשָׂמִים.

Baruch Atah Adonai,
Eloheinu Melech ha'olam,
Borei minei v'samim.

Blessed are You,
Adonai our God,
Ruler of the World.
Who creates
fragrant spices.

Smell the spices.

Light candle and raise cup of wine:

בָּרוּךְ אַתָּה יְיָ
אֱלֹהֵינוּ מֶלֶךְ הָעוֹלָם
בּוֹרֵא פְּרִי הַגָּפֶן.

Baruch Atah Adonai,
Eloheinu Melech ha'olam,
Borei p'ri hagafen.

Blessed are You,
Adonai our God,
Ruler of the World.
Who creates the
fruit of the vine.

Raise candle:

בָּרוּךְ אַתָּה יְיָ
אֱלֹהֵינוּ מֶלֶךְ הָעוֹלָם
בּוֹרֵא מְאוֹרֵי הָאֵשׁ.

Baruch Atah Adonai,
Eloheinu Melech ha'olam,
Borei m'orei ha'esh.

Blessed are You,
Adonai our God,
Ruler of the World.
Who creates the
lights of fire.

Blessed are You, Adonai our God, Who makes things different.

You make the holy different from the everyday,
Light different from darkness,
The Jewish people different from other people,
And Shabbat different from the rest of the week.

בָּרוּךְ אַתָּה יְיָ הַמַבְדִּיל בֵּין קֹדֶשׁ לְחוֹל.

Baruch Atah Adonai, hamavdil bein kodesh l'chol.

Blessed are You Adonai,
Who makes the holy different from the everyday.

Drink the wine.

We hope a time comes when every day is as sweet as
Shabbat. At Havdalah we look to the teachings of Elijah,
a great prophet, to help us bring that day closer.

We sing.

Eliyahu hanavi, Eliyahu hatishbi.
Eliyahu, Eliyahu, Eliyahu hagiladi.
Bimhera v'yameinu yavo eleinu im Mashiach ben David.

May Elijah the Prophet come quickly and in our day,
bringing the time of Messiah.

Shavua Tov.

ABOUT THE SERVICE

This service is designed for young families to use either in the synagogue or at home. It may be used on Friday night or Saturday and takes about 15 minutes, including an opening and closing song, but not including a Torah service or storytime. There is also a brief *Havdalah* service to end Shabbat.

The prayers chosen focus on the central themes of a traditional Shabbat service:

• Shabbat is a special day, different from the rest of the week. We make it special by doing different things, or doing things in a different way. For example, during the week we eat all kinds of bread; on Shabbat we eat challah. During the week we read all kinds of books; on Shabbat we read stories from the Torah. On Shabbat we say special prayers. Shabbat is a time for families.

• Shabbat is a time to think about the past and the future, a time to put things in perspective.

• Shabbat is a time when we remember creation, revelation (Torah), and redemption (exodus from slavery in Egypt).

This service follows the basic structure of the worship service. The following analogy may help to explain it:

When we make friends, we do it in stages. First we find out enough about the other person to decide we'd like to become friends. Then, we find out if we can depend on the other person. As time goes by we find out more, and if we are really good friends, we make plans for the future.

A Shabbat service takes us through those same stages. Only this time, the friend we come close to is God. When we say the Shema, we say we would like to be close to God. When we say the Amidah, we talk about the ways we can depend on God. When we read the Torah, we find out more about God. And when we say the Aleinu, we plan our future with God.

The following are ideas to involve children in the service:

• Encourage them to participate in traditional movements that accompany certain prayers, such as facing the door to welcome Shabbat in *L'cha Dodi*, and bowing for the *Barechu* and *Va'anachnu kor'im*.

• Select from the personal prayers included in the Torah service. Shabbat is a time for the community to celebrate happy and sad moments together. Call on children who will be celebrating a birthday to say *Shehecheyanu*. Invite them to recite names of family and friends who are ill and to say a prayer for their good health. Check a Jewish calendar and if a new month is coming, recite the blessing for a new moon and talk about the holidays that will be celebrated.

• When introducing the *Kaddish*, pause so parents and children can call to mind someone who has died and remember the happy times they spent together.

• Sing *Adon Olam* (and other songs) to a tune which calls for the congregation to echo the leader, so young children can join in. You may also want to teach children to use sign language or other movements while they sing.